KU-518-950

INSIDE...

Published 2020

Little Brother Books Ltd,
Ground Floor, 23 Southernhay
East, Exeter, Devon, EX1 1QL

Printed in the UK

books@littlebrotherbooks.co.uk
www.littlebrotherbooks.co.uk

LittleBrother
B O O K S

THE HISTORY OF MINECRAFT

Years ago, Swedish game developer Markus 'Notch' Persson was working on a game called RubyDung when he came across Zach Barth's Infiniminer.

He realised that this was just the kind of game he wanted to do, a first-person sandbox game that allowed players to create anything they could dream of. In a short time his studio Mojang whipped up an engine in Java that looks almost exactly like Minecraft does today!

The first Minecraft Alpha opened on June 13th, 2009. A month later there were over 20,000 registered players, and Minecraft was up and running. A Survival mode was soon added to the game, and regular Friday updates began introducing all sorts of new features that are now standard. These included dungeons, minecarts, and The Nether.

The game was more of a huge hit than anyone could have predicted. By January 2011 there were over one million Minecraft player accounts registered. By July 2011 it was 10 million!

Players became obsessed with the game. Teams of modders added skins and levels by the thousands, creating masterpieces no one could have ever imagined were possible. Version 1.0 hit in November 2011 with The End, a section that finally gave the game a finale. It was closure for Notch too, who stepped down from the project and let coder Jens 'Jeb' Bergensten take over as lead.

A mobile edition of Minecraft was followed by various console editions, and the amount of players just grew and grew.

Minecraft has since gone on to become the best-selling video game of all time. Not too bad for a little Swedish studio!

WHAT IS MINECRAFT?

Minecraft is essentially a massive sandbox game that allows you to create almost anything you want. You can build your own blocky creations, fight off monsters, hang out with friends, or just explore worlds! So what do you do?

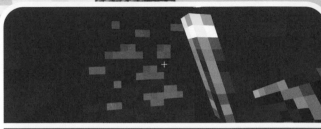

MINE

It's in the name, so of course mining is a big part of the game. Armed with your trusty pickaxe (or just your bare hands), you can knock apart the blocks of a world to collect items for making your own creations.

BUILD

Once you've mined some resources you can get started on your own builds. There are all sorts of types of blocks to find and place, allowing you to create literally anything that you can imagine.

CRAFT

Filling your inventory with items is great, but unless you learn how to craft you won't unlock the true potential of the game. Items can be combined to make new, better items, including tools that help you mine or fight enemies.

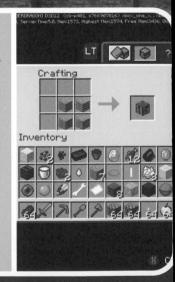

SMELT AND ENHANCE

Why stop at crafting? Using items such as furnaces and anvils you can modify tools and weapons to make them even better.

MEET MOBS

'Mob' is short for 'mobile', and it means any creature in the game. That can be anything from friendly villagers you can trade with to deadly zombies that want a piece of you. Keep a sword on hand for these encounters!

LEVEL UP

Experience (or XP for short) is usually earned by killing monsters or mining resources, although you can get it for other activities, like fishing and trading. Unlike in other games, gaining XP doesn't level up your character's abilities, but you can use it to enchant or repair items.

CHANGE YOUR LOOK

You can equip your avatar with different skins to change its look. Players can buy skins or make their own custom creations, allowing them to sport very unique looks.

THREE WAYS TO PLAY MINECRAFT

1

SURVIVAL MODE

As the name suggests, survival is the name of the game! You start this mode with absolutely nothing and have to mine and construct some shelter before night descends on the world. That's when hostile mobs come to attack you in the dark. Die and you'll lose everything you have!

CREATIVE MODE

2

Creative mode allows you to just focus on building. You won't have to worry about hostile mobs or mining. It gives you absolutely everything you could ever hope to find in the game and even lets you fly around the world to build up into the sky!

3

ADVENTURE MODE

This mode offers player-created maps that are intended for specific adventures. Here you'll find all kinds of amazing mini-games and even full-featured stories that have been crafted for your enjoyment. You can't destroy or place any blocks, making sure that no one can break the world and spoil things.

Never. Stop. Building.

There are so many editions of Minecraft, you'll be able to work on your virtual world no matter where you are in the real world!

There are so many different versions of Minecraft available right now, the biggest problem may be figuring out which one to get! The good news is you really can't go wrong no matter which you pick, since even the mobile versions have much of the same functionality as the others. The best idea may simply be to choose whichever platform you play on the most, or grab one for your home base and one for when you're on the go.

The good news is that no matter where you are, you'll always be somewhere that you can play Minecraft.

Fortunately Minecraft also supports online cross-platform play for up to eight players! That means that you can team up with your friends no matter if they're on PC, Android or iOS devices, Xbox One, Nintendo Switch, or even Oculus Rift. You can all join forces, building and exploring the world as a team.

CONSOLES YOU CAN PLAY MINECRAFT ON:

Xbox One
Xbox 360
Nintendo 3DS
Wii U
Nintendo Switch
PlayStation 3
PlayStation 4
PlayStation Vita

EDITIONS YOU DIDN'T KNOW EXISTED!

Amazon Fire
Fire TV
Oculus Rift
Gear VR
Raspberry Pi

VERSIONS OF MINECRAFT:

Minecraft: Java Edition (PC/Mac/Linux)
Minecraft: Windows 10 Edition (PC)
Minecraft Classic (PC)
Minecraft 4K (PC)
Minecraft Education Edition (PC)
Minecraft (formerly Pocket Edition) (iOS, Android)

JAVA VS BEDROCK:

In 2017 the Better Together Update made Minecraft a cross-platform game, allowing you to play with friends on other versions. They called this the Bedrock Edition, although it's just titled Minecraft now.

This update also retitled the original PC version to Minecraft: Java Edition. The Java Edition is the only way to play with user-created skins and mods!

DISCONTINUED VERSIONS:

These versions are either not being updated or have new Bedrock versions replacing them!

Xbox One
Xbox 360
Nintendo Switch
Wii U
PlayStation 3
PlayStation 4
PlayStation Vita

MINECRAFT REALMS

There are two different versions of Realms for different platforms – Minecraft Realms Plus and Minecraft Realms: Java Edition. Players on the Java Edition can only play with each other.

WHAT ARE REALMS?

Realms are personal servers for you and your friends. Having your own private server is really cool, because it means that your world is always accessible, even when you're not playing! You can make sure that only people you invite can enter your world and they don't even need a subscription to join your Realm. You can also customise your Realm however you like.

SO WHAT IS REALMS PLUS?

This is Minecraft's subscription service, which costs £5.99 a month to keep your content. You do get your first month for free to try it out, though. Note that Realms Plus is only available for Minecraft on Xbox One, Nintendo Switch, mobile, Windows 10, and Amazon Fire.

COOL CONTENT!

As well as your very own Realm the other big bonus is that you get 50 pieces of content to enjoy right away, such as adventures, mini-games, worlds and skin packs. There's new content to enjoy every month, but if you ever end your subscription, you won't have access to it anymore!

BLOCKS UPON BLOCKS

Blocks are literally the building blocks of Minecraft. Without them, there would be no game. You will mine and place thousands of cubes while playing the game, so it's important to know all about them.

Each block is about a cubic meter square, which works out to 16x16x16 pixels on a screen. However, there are high-res texture packs available that can make blocks look a bit more pleasing to the eye.

There are over 150 types of blocks to play around with in Minecraft, but each is one of three types:

TRANSPARENT

SEMI-TRANSPARENT

OPAQUE

BLOCKS OF THE NATURAL WORLD

These blocks are found throughout the world and can be mined to make all sorts of things. Here are some of the more common ones:

DIRT: Just plain dirt.

SAND: Sand. Lots of sand.

STONE: Mining this turns it into cobblestone.

WOOD: One of the most important blocks for starting crafting.

BEDROCK: The indestructible block that prevents you from digging to the centre of the Earth.

COAL ORE: You'll need to mine ore with a pickaxe, and this block type is the most common.

GOLD ORE: Gold is found deep underground, but is more common than you'd expect in Minecraft!

OBSIDIAN: Created where lava and water meet.

LAPIS LAZULI: If you want enchantments, you'll need to keep an eye out for this blue and grey block

EMERALD ORE: The rarest ore in the game!

DRAGON EGG: The Ender Dragon spawns this on top of the exit portal. Get to The End to find it...

BUILDING BLOCKS

These blocks don't exist unless you make them. This is usually done by using a furnace or crafting table.

GLASS

Melt sand in a furnace to get this transparent block. Even though you can see through it, most monsters can't.

JACK-O-LANTERN

Torches are booooring. Combine a torch with a pumpkin for this stylish light. They even shine underwater!

BRICK

Bake a clay ball in a furnace to produce bricks. Craft four bricks together and you'll get these invaluable blocks for building a home.

SNOW

Combine four snowballs for one of these, a cold yet tough block that won't melt near fire.

FENCE

These crafted blocks are the size of 1 ¼ normal blocks, and are big enough to keep mobs from entering an area. Good to keep farm animals contained!

STAIRS

Stop jumping all over town by placing some of these around. You can make them out of everything from wood to brick.

PRO TIP

When you build a house, try using a variety of blocks. A house made solely of bricks or stone is ugly as can be!

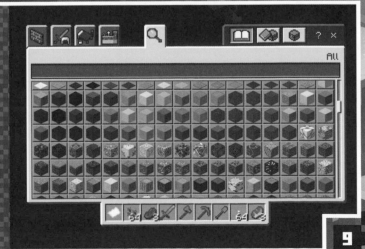

UTILITY BLOCKS

You make these blocks yourself, but they do more than just look neat. They actually have all kinds of uses!

FURNACE

Use these to cook food and melt materials. Hardcore builders will really need one!

ENCHANTMENT TABLE

You know all that XP you've been earning? You can use it with this table to enchant all sorts of gear!

CRAFTING TABLE

You'll need these to craft most of the best items in the game. It gives you six crafting spots versus the four the inventory has.

LADDER

Get to the top of your structure in style!

DOORS

Keep out mobs with these.

CHEST

Too much stuff? Craft a chest and you'll have a place to stick 27 items in it. If you place two chests next to each other, you'll make a wider chest.

PRESSURE PLATES

Stand on these and you'll activate a mechanism of your own design. Mobs can set them off too, which makes them perfect for traps!

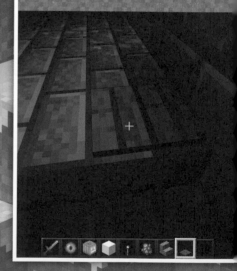

BEDS

How else are you supposed to get some rest in this game?

THE NETHER

Stepped on a portal by accident and ended up in The Nether? It happens. This region has blocks that don't exist anywhere else, and is far more dangerous than the Overworld. Die here and you'll end up back home, but your items will stay behind.

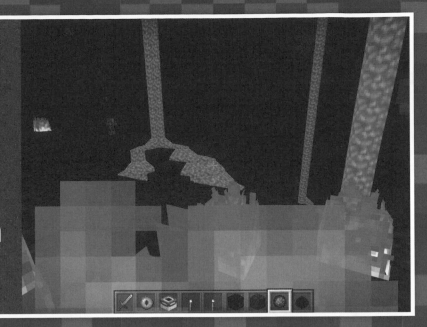

NETHERRACK

These stones will burn and burn and never go out until you do it yourself. They're really useful for a fiery defensive perimeter!

NETHERBRICK

These are everywhere in this biome. Mine the blocks to craft tough stairs and fences.

SOUL SAND

Basically quicksand, this sand will slow players and mobs down, causing them to sink into it.

GLOWSTONE

These blocks are some of the only sources of light in the Nether. They can be used as chandeliers!

DID YOU KNOW?

The only types of blocks in the game you can't build are air and water.

Diamonds can only be mined with an iron or diamond pickaxe.

CRAFTING!

A GUIDE TO BASIC RECIPES

Minecraft is all about being creative. As such, you'll need to know a few basic recipes to make important items. These are the things you should build, in order.

CRAFTING TABLE

Firstly, craft any type of wooden blocks into planks. Then use four wood planks to create a crafting table. Now you're all set to craft blocks and items. Place the table anywhere in the world and click on it to open it up.

NEXT STEPS

BASIC ITEMS

Now grab some wooden planks and sticks and get crafting. These basic tools and weapons are essential items you'll need in order to mine other materials, but they are quite weak to start off with. Make them stronger and you're then able to use them to mine for even more handy resources.

PICKAXE
Needed to mine ore.

SHOVEL
Handy for digging deep into the ground.

AXE
This will greatly reduce the time it takes to chop down trees.

SWORD
You'll need something to fight off mobs at night.

GET FIRED UP
The next step is to build a furnace to make more Minecraft items! Construct this from eight cobblestone blocks. It's used to cook food and smelt objects to make new items.

IRON ORE Smelts into Iron Ingot.

GOLD ORE Smelts into Gold Ingot.

WOOD Smelts into Charcoal.

SAND Smelts into Glass.

RAW FOOD Cooks into Cooked Food.

COBBLESTONE Smelts into Stone.

CACTI Smelts into Cactus Green.

NETHERRACK Smelts into Nether Brick.

CLAY Smelts into Bricks.

ENCHANTMENTS

POWER – Increases arrow damage for all you aspiring Robin Hoods.

MENDING – Want to keep a broken item? Mend it with this enchantment.

LOOTING – Causes mobs to drop more items!

KNOCKBACK – Increases how far you hit enemies back with your sword.

EFFICIENCY – Mine much faster with this useful enchantment.

UNBREAKING – The item's durability will be greatly enhanced.

THORNS – Hurts anyone who dares to touch you with a melee attack!

ENCHANTING ENCHANTMENTS!
Craft an enchanting table and magically enhance tools and weapons, giving them special abilities. To make an enchanting table, place one book, two diamonds and four obsidian into the 3x3 crafting grid as shown above. Once crafted, add it to your inventory. Whenever you want to enchant an item, it will costs you XP and lapis lazuli.

GET BREWING
You can make potions using a brwewing stand made from one Blaze Rod and three cobblestones, as shown above. Combine with Blaze Powder, a glass bottle, water and various ingredients to make different potions.

POTIONS

HEALING – Something everyone can use, especially in Survival mode.

FIRE RESISTANCE – You'll want these before heading over to The Nether.

NIGHT VISION – Use this if you're heading underground. Works underwater, too!

STRENGTH – Get ready to fight off enemies with this potion, which makes you super strong.

REGENERATION – Heals you over time.

GET BUILDING!

While it's entirely possible to build anything you can imagine in Survival mode, however Creative mode is the best place to try making massive creations. Why not start with your first home?

ADVANTAGES IN CREATIVE MODE

You build much faster in Creative mode, as one click removes or places a block.

Hostile mobs won't bother you. Also, if you die, you won't lose any of your items.

You have the gift of flight! Jump twice and you can soar high into the air.

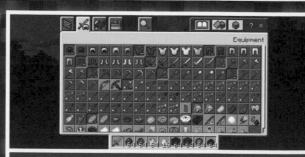

You don't need to collect items – you have access to unlimited resources.

HOUSE PLANS

Before you start building, decide what you what to construct. What shape will it be? This will help you choose how to begin.

1

LAY A FOUNDATION
You have to start from the ground and work your way up. Outline your structure with cobblestone, leaving room for at least one door, and digging down if you want a basement.

2

MAKE A FRAME
Start with the corners and build the frame to your structure! That will allow you to lay floors and stairs for the higher levels.

3

ADD WINDOWS
Add windows so you can get some light into your home. Recess them from the walls, because otherwise they might look a little bit silly.

Glass Pane

4

BEAUTIFY!
Once you're done with the basic building, it's time to start adding some flair to (and around) it. Torches for light, flower beds for beauty, trees for shade. Keep adding details until your plain building becomes something remarkable!

DECORATE YOUR HOME
No one wants to live in an empty building, do they? Now's the time to add stuff to your house to make it truly feel like home!

DECIDE WHAT EACH ROOM IS
Is this the kitchen? Add a stove and fridge! What about adding a bed and bookshelves to your bedroom? If you create a living room you can hang paintings or banners, and even add chairs and tables. Including these items will also let people immediately identify where they are in your home.

FUNCTIONAL ITEMS
There are plenty of items available that not only look great, but they actually do something! Why place a simple torch when you can hang a chandelier? Why make a plain glass window when you can create beautiful stained glass? Jukeboxes can add music to a home, and filling a workshop with the essentials (such as a crafting table, furnace, chest) means never having to travel to make new items.

BUILDING PORTALS!

It may seem like you wouldn't want to go to The Nether or End realms, since they're so dangerous and dismal, but if you're curious about what these otherworldly lands look like, there's an easy way. Make a portal!

It's easy to try building a portal in Creative mode, because you are given everything you need to make one.

NETHER PORTAL

Nether portals are built as upright rectangular frames made from 14 blocks of obsidian and opened with fire – appropriate for the place they're going to send you.

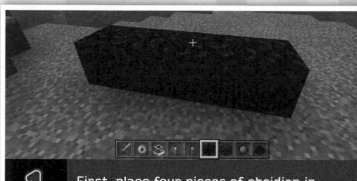

1 First, place four pieces of obsidian in a row on the ground.

3 Finish the top of the frame to complete it.

4

The last step is to simply ignite the portal by using a fire of some sort. Regular old flint and steel will work, although you can do it in style with the fire charge or blaze fireball.

Now you just jump through it and end up in the hellish dimension! Good luck...

2 Now build the sides up to five blocks high.

PRO TIPS:
- You can actually construct the frame without the four corner pieces, letting you build it much faster in Creative mode!
- You can't build a Nether Portal in the End, so don't even try.

THE END PORTAL

Want to see what The End Game looks like? Find a portal by using flying Eyes of Ender to guide you. These will float in the direction of a stronghold containing the portal. Or you can just build your own portal!

1

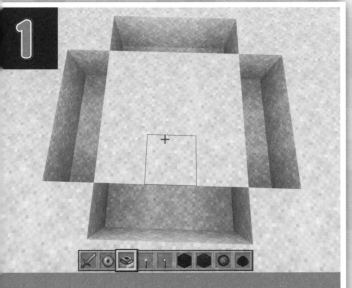

First, dig the holes in the ground. It's a five by five square with the corners cut off.

2

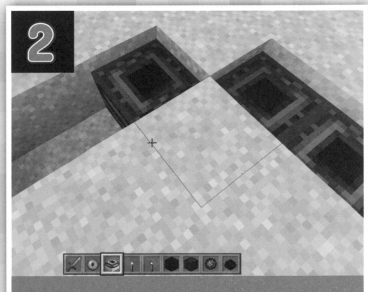

Then fill the holes with End portal frames, but make sure they're all facing the same direction.

3

Fill the End portal frames with Eyes of Ender, making sure they're all facing the same way as the End portals. If any are sideways, then the portal won't open!

4

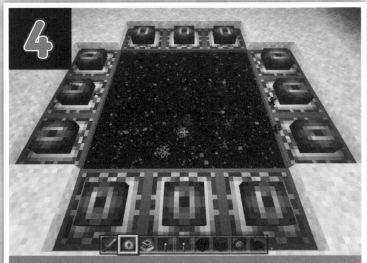

The portal will emerge in the ground, allowing you to dive in and face the Ender Dragon in the epic final battle of the game!

FINDING THE PERFECT BIOME FOR YOUR NEW HOME

A biome is the climate zone of each region, separating each world into different sections. Working in Creative Mode allows you to choose which one you'd like to build upon! Each biome has sub-biomes with different styles such as mountains, snow, and more. Try and pick one that fits the theme of what you're trying to build. These are just some of the types you can find!

SNOWY BIOMES

SNOWY TUNDRA
Don't expect many trees here. These biomes are flat and full of snow.

ICE PLAINS
If snow and frozen landscapes are your thing, then this is the place to build your amazing creations.

COLD BIOMES

TAIGA
These are flat biomes with plenty of trees and tall grass. There are Snowy, Mountainous, and Giant Tree Taiga versions as well. Wolves and foxes live here!

OCEAN BIOMES

OCEAN
There's not much land to build on here, of course. But you can make an amazing undersea palace – provided you have plenty of sponges after you've crafted it and sealed it up.

EMPERATE/LUSH BIOMES

FOREST
Want to build a treehouse? You'll find plenty of wood here.

SWAMP
Lots of water and islands for you to explore. Perfect for a hidden pirate cove!

JUNGLE
Welcome to the jungle! It's got everything you could want, as long as that's huts, jungle mobs, and lost temples.

PLAINS
This is what you think of when you play Minecraft. It's flat, has plenty of grass, and looks perfect for a farm or house.

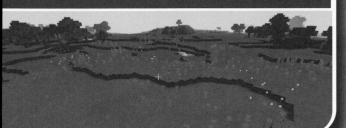

MUSHROOM ISLAND
The ideal setting for a fantasy world. With its strange plants and giant red mushrooms, it's easily the weirdest of them all!

RY/WARM BIOMES

SAVANNA
You can go on safari here! It's a flat biome full of acacia wood, where horses and llamas will spawn.

DESERT
Sand. Some may hate the way it gets everywhere, but how else are you going to build a pyramid for a home?

BADLANDS
If you want to build a saloon in a Wild West setting, here's your biome. The canyons and red sand give it a unique look.

THE END BIOMES

THE END
This is it. This biome has one giant island surrounded by a group of smaller ones, which are surrounded by nothing but the void. There's no day, no night. Just weak light. Good luck...

NETHER WASTES
This is a dangerous, fiery place. It's dark and the only lights are things like lava and glowstone. Want to be overlord of your own dimension? Build a massive castle right here.

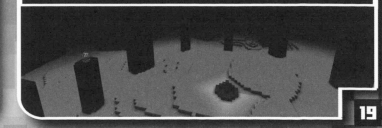

PROTECTING YOUR CASTLE

When choosing your home it's all about location, location, location. This is doubly important in Survival mode, where you're going to need to fight off roving hordes of monsters every single night. Picking the right spot for your home could mean the difference between life and death!

STARTER HOME
When you first start the game, your best bet may be to use the natural environment to your advantage. You won't have enough time before darkness sets to make a decent home, so dig into a mountain or a cave and you'll have strong rock protecting you for the first night. Just make sure there's nothing lurking in the shadows and get ready to build in the daylight!

BUILDING TIPS
Creepers can blow up your home, keep them away by building trenches or a moat. Creepers' explosions don't hurt as much when they're in water, so take advantage of this and fight them where it won't damage your creation.

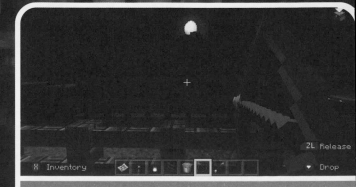

DO FENCE ME IN
You can place a fence all around your home that will at the very least slow mobs down. Most won't be able to climb over them and you'll be able to hear them coming, so place them all around for some easy defences.

BRIGHTEN THINGS UP

Hostile mobs mostly hate the light, so they'll shy away if it's too bright. Try to place torches and jack-o-lanterns all around your house, or just build it with a lot of glowstone blocks! Plus, it will look awesome at night...

TOWER OVER YOUR ENEMIES

Build a sniper tower and pick your enemies off from a distance with a bow before they get anywhere close to damaging you. Another good idea is to place snow golems up on top of additional towers to protect you!

GET TRAPPED

If you want to be even more proactive, set up traps that eliminate hostile mobs so you don't have to. Fill dispensers with arrows or fire charges to shoot at anyone who approaches. Or create a minefield all around your home by digging holes in the ground and laying TNT underneath. Wire the explosives to pressure plates with redstone dust so anyone who steps on them will go boom. Just make sure to mark them so you don't get caught in your own traps!

MAKE IT IMPOSSIBLE

Feel like being completely isolated? Make a home that you have to enter through a hole in the basement, so intricate that it's hard for anyone to get into. Or even try making an underwater home, where no mobs will be able to touch you!

ZOMBIE-PROOF DOORS

Use iron doors instead of wooden ones. They're much harder to make but zombies can't break them down, unlike wooden doors which they can easily smash in.

BEWARE THE MONSTERS!

HOSTILE MOBS

While Minecraft may seem like a bright and happy land, when the sun sets things change! Hostile mobs roam the land, seeking helpless villages to attack. There are all sorts of dangerous creatures on the prowl. Here are some to watch for.

CREEPER

These are almost the mascots of Minecraft. The little green monsters explode and can easily take apart your well-designed home. Try to destroy them at a distance with a bow.

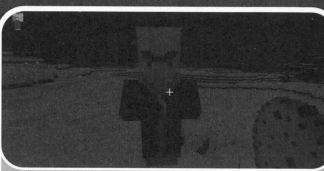

EVOKER

These 'illagers' were thrown out of towns and went off to live in intricate buildings to practice dark magic. These evildoers can materialise ghostly fang traps that can bite you from the ground. Evokers can also summon the Vex, tough flying imps that swoop down and attack with iron swords.

GUARDIAN

Guardians can be found inside ocean temples, making it dangerous to go diving. Elder Guardians are twice as large and twice as dangerous. They drop lots of good loot if you manage to take them down, though!

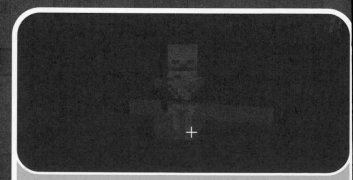

SKELETON

Fairly weak, skeletons can still be a threat because they attack from a distance with a bow. Sometimes the first thing you'll know about a nearby skeleton is the twang of a bow. Try to get them to hit another mob by accident – they'll both fight and leave you alone. Some skeletons ride horses or spiders!

VINDICATOR

Kicked out of their villages just like the Evokers, they have their own homes in the woods. They aren't that tough but they are fierce fighters, especially when they're in a group. Watch out for those axes!

WITCH

These evil beings laugh at you as they throw potions that cause you to become slowed, poisoned, or weakened. What's more, they can make potions to protect against fire and water and even heal themselves! A drink of milk can help clear up your ailments as you take on any witches.

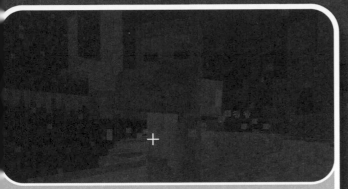

ZOMBIE

The most common hostile mob. They are slow and you can always hear them coming, thanks to their loud groans. They're not much of a threat unless you underestimate them though. They were once villagers, so help put them out of their misery.

NETHER MOBS

Step through a Nether portal and you'll end up in this dangerous, molten land. If the lava everywhere wasn't bad enough, there are hostile mobs roaming the land. Make sure you're equipped with diamond gear before heading off there.

BLAZE

It may look like this mob is on fire, but it's actually a yellow block with flame rods around it. Blazes shoot off fireballs, making them difficult to fight without the use of fire resistance. The best weapon against them? Just try using the lowly snowball...

GHAST

This huge creature spits out fireballs that explode on impact. They can also destroy your portal and leave you stranded in the Nether. But kill one and you might get lucky with Ghast tears, which when brewed with awkward potion, makes a regeneration potion.

MAGMA CUBE

These flaming cubes can be a small, medium or large block. When they move they spring to a great height and will try to squash you as they jump around.

WITHER SKELETON

What's so scary about these? You've likely faced hundreds of skeletons before getting to the Nether, after all. Well these skeletons are gigantic and fast, and their attacks can infect you with Wither, which causes you to slowly die. Their skulls can help you summon a Wither, if you dare...

ZOMBIE PIGMAN

Half-pig, half-man, all-zombie. They are actually peaceful, unless you mess with them, in which case they will stop at nothing to get you. It might be worth fighting this gnarly beast, though, as they always carry a lot of gold items, everything from nuggets to swords and ingots.

MOBS AT THE END

The End is a scary, desolate place. It's mostly made up of deserted islands floating above a black void, but it's also home to some dangerous mobs.

ENDERMAN

Yep, these show up here, too. Wear a carved pumpkin or quaff an invisibility potion and they won't bother with you as long as you leave them well alone.

SHULKER

These creatures are hard to spot, as they look similar to the purpur blocks in The End. It shoots slow homing magic missiles that do a ton of damage and lifts victims into the air, leaving them prone to fall damage! Shulker shells protect them from attacks, so wait until it's open and then attack. Defeated Shulkers can sometimes drop their shell, which can be crafted into a tough box when combined with a chest.

BOSS MOBS

By far the most dangerous mobs you'll encounter, don't fight these beasts unless you're really well-prepared. It's worth it though if you do, as they'll drop all kinds of cool treasure.

THE WITHER

This three-headed monster can be spawned by using four blocks of soul sand (or soul soil) and three Wither Skeleton skulls. It explodes when it first spawns, catching unsuspecting players by surprise. It has 300 health points and is immune to fire and drowning.

Each of its heads launches skull projectiles, allowing it to hit multiple players at the same time. Anything they hit gets inflicted with the Wither Effect, which drains your health for 40 seconds. Defeat it you'll earn a Nether Star, which can be turned into a beacon!

THE ENDER DRAGON

Only a few have been able to survive a battle with this mob. It spawns when you first enter The End – you'll see it flying over the main island, which is also home to lots of Enderman!

The huge creature attacks with toxic breath and damaging fireballs, so stock up on health and regeneration potions. The Dragon can heal itself from crystals on top of the obsidian pillars, so build your way up to destroy them. Defeat it and 12,000 XP will be yours, as well as the Ender Dragon Egg.

UTILITY MOBS

This all sounds dangerous, right, but why fight by yourself? Simply construct these powerful golems and they'll help you in battle!

IRON GOLEM

These iron giants can be found patrolling villages, protecting them from roaming zombies with ease, or sloppy players who accidentally hurt villagers. You can construct your own iron golem with four iron blocks arranged in a T-shape, with a pumpkin placed on top of the middle block. Attach it to a lead and it will follow you wherever you go.

SNOW GOLEM

Very similar to the iron golem, but weaker. It leaves behind a layer of snow, allowing you to craft snowballs no matter where you are. It's very weak against enemy attacks (a wooden sword will kill it in one swipe!) and fire. So you probably want to keep it far from the Nether, as handy as snowballs may seem there.

MOB SCENE

For all the mobs that can harm you, there are plenty of mobs that are just living their lives. These neutral and passive mobs can still be of use, as they provide valuable items!

BATS

Bats get scared very easily if you run across them in caves, so it's hard to track them down. They're super easy to kill but drop nothing, so best to leave them alone. They're bad pets too, since they'll often just fly away!

BEES

The latest addition to Minecraft. They fly around pollinating plants (which then advance to their next growth stage with the bee's help) and living happy little bee lives. While they'll leave you alone, don't mess with a hive unless you want a real fight – they will poison you.

CHICKENS

They lay eggs every five to ten minutes. You can cook with eggs, making cakes and pies. There's also a one in eight chance that throwing an egg will cause a chick to hatch! Plus, you can kill them for feathers and meat. Note: unlike other meats you should never eat a raw chicken, as it may cause food poisoning. Always cook your chicken!

COWS

Cows are really useful farm animals, so it's a good idea to collect a herd. Use a bucket on them to obtain milk, which can cure all effects, good or bad. They can also drop leather that can be made into equipment like hats and boots. Plus, they're a good source of steak!

PIGS

Have you found a saddle on your travels? If so you can put one on a pig and ride it around! Use a fishing rod and carrot together to create a carrot on a stick, which you can use to guide your pink friend where to go. Plus, if you're ever in the mood for pork chops, here's where you'll find them.

RABBITS

Rabbits drop hides and meat, both of which are really useful. Four hides can be crafted into leather, and their meat can be cooked into a delicious stew with a bowl, mushroom, carrot, and baked potato. Yum, yum!

SHEEP

If you want wool, you'll need to capture a few of these. Killing a sheep nets you a block of wool, but if you use shears (crafted with two iron ingots) you'll end up with one to three blocks of wool, and a naked sheep. Its wool will grow back, allowing you to shear it again.

SQUID

They may look scary, but squids are completely harmless. If they are killed they drop ink sacs, a necessity for dying things black. If they end up beached on land they will quickly die, so if you want to hang on to them, keep them wet.

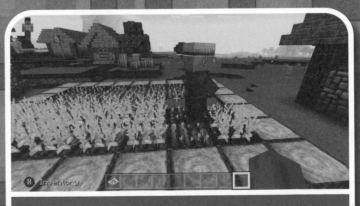

VILLAGERS

These are people living in town that can help you out. They wear different clothes depending on their jobs, and will trade items with you. The more you trade with them, the more they'll trust you and offer you deals. Keep these people safe from roving mobs!

WORKING WITH FRIENDS

As fun as Minecraft is by yourself, it's much more fun with friends. You can choose to build intricate creations together, make up your own multiplayer games, or even fight to the death!

Multiplayer Settings

- Multiplayer Game

Microsoft Account Settings

- Invite Only
- Friends Only
- Friends of Friends

ON OR OFF THE COUCH

First you'll have to figure out where to play. Minecraft allows console users to play local split screen co-op with real-life friends, but it also allows you to play together online. Start a server and choose to make it public or private, inviting players to join your world on your own terms.

Chat and Commands

< Back

Press T or RETURN to open chat
Dragonepic10137 » almond where r u
TicK Critick » XD
» You have been hidden. (Hidden Zone)
» You are now visible.
AlmondThread328 » XD
TicK Critick » Lol
[!] Follow our Twitter: @theHiveMC
Dragonepic10137 » where r u almond
NaiveCookie8141 » me banean porfa
TicK Critick » Bruh
Dragonepic10137 » r u almond
TicK Critick » xd
AlmondThread328 » right here
hxcking6blocks » does anyone want to play Treasure Wars?
GIOVALOL43 » lol

sure I will!

COMMUNICATION IS KEY

Take advantage of the in-game chat to better collaborate. Rather than just running around building things with no plan, discuss exactly what you want to do. All of the players can then choose different portions of the project and get things done that much faster.

SURVIVE TOGETHER

When playing in Survival mode, Minecraft's difficulty will automatically scale to the number of players. That means if more friends join your game the mobs will become much more dangerous, but if someone drops out it becomes much easier. You'll be able to set up defences as a team, and choose different roles for each player. Have someone hang back with ranged attacks and someone all armoured up and ready for melee combat!

Plus, some of the most famous servers allow for mini-games that completely change the Minecraft experience. You can find team-based capture the flag games, zombie horde survival games, or even games that mimic other video games, such as Grand Theft Auto and Pokémon.

Game Over!   ✕

Your game overview:

➤ 58 Experience
➤ 4 Checkpoints Hit
➤ 0 Kills
➤ 17 Deaths

We'll find a new game shortly...

| **Close Overview** |
| **Exit to Hub** |

PLAY TOGETHER

If you play online you can find game servers that have recreations of some of your favourite fictional lands to visit. Ever wanted to go to (blocky versions of) Westeros, Skyrim, or Arkham Prison? You can find almost anything here, and if you can't, just start a server and make your own!

You normally can't fight other players in Minecraft, but if PvP (Player Vs Player) is enabled on the server, all bets are off. Defeat other players and their inventory will drop to the ground, offering plenty of loot! If you organise it well you can fight in teams or just one-on-one.

PREPARE FOR COMBAT

Of course, you don't have to work together. Instead of cooperating, you can always just choose to fight other players!

Adopt A Pet

You can tame wild animals and make them into your best friends, or even get a bunch and make your very own pack! Here are some of the best animals you can find, and how to go about taming them.

DOGS

The dogs you'll find in Minecraft are actually wild wolves. Look for Forest or Taiga biomes (the only places they spawn) and explore the woods until you find one. Make sure you have a bone in hand, as you'll need it! The easiest way to get a bone is to destroy a skeleton. They're pretty common and can frequently be found in chests. Walk up to the wolf and feed it a bone. It might take a couple of attempts before it eats it, but you'll now have a faithful canine companion.

PUPPIES

Want more dogs? Get two dogs and you'll be able to breed them! If you have two dog companions, you just have to feed them in order to encourage them to make baby wolves.

They'll eat any meat you have on you, and it can be raw too – dogs don't discriminate. Dogs also heal from being fed meat. Make sure you have lots of extra food in your inventory, as you'll have to keep the new puppies fed. Get really crazy and you can become the leader of an entire pack – 16 dogs that will follow you and hunt their own food. They will attack any nearby enemies, and they absolutely terrify Skeletons, who look like one big delicious stack of bones to dogs!

CATS

Stray cats spawn in villages, while wild cats (ocelots) can be found in Jungle biomes. Cats are more picky than dogs, and will only take raw fish, so stock up.

You'll have to befriend the wild cats first, as they're very skittish. Walk up to them slowly and don't make any quick movements, or the cat will run away. When the cat is ready to be fed it will walk slowly up to you. Feed it and you'll tame it, changing it to a different look.

KITTIES!

You need two tame cats (or ocelots) to breed. Feed them uncooked fish and they'll fall in love (hearts will appear over their head). You'll have kittens in no time, so have some more fish ready to go.

Your new pets will hang out in your home, sitting on your bed or even on your chests. They can get in the way of your stuff and you'll need to push the cat off to open chests! Cats won't hunt food like dogs, but Creepers and Phantoms are scared of them and won't come near, so it's handy to have a couple on hand to keep monsters away!

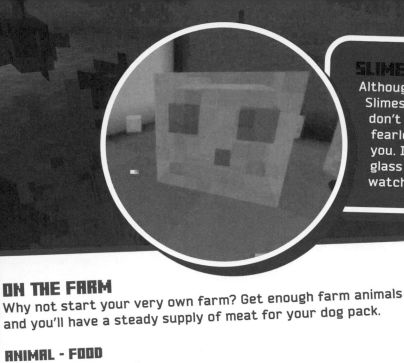

SLIMES

Although Slimes are hostile mobs, tiny Slimes have zero attack damage and don't need taming. They are absolutely fearless, and will attack any enemy for you. If you like you can make a little glass home for them, where you can watch them jump around all happy-like.

ON THE FARM

Why not start your very own farm? Get enough farm animals and you'll have a steady supply of meat for your dog pack.

ANIMAL - FOOD

Sheep – Grass, wheat
Cows – Wheat
Llamas – Hay bales, wheat
Rabbits – Golden carrots, carrots, dandelions
Parrots – Wheat seeds, beetroot seeds, melon seeds, pumpkin seeds
Horses/Donkeys/Mules – Golden apples, apples, sugar, wheat, hay bales
Chickens – Wheat seeds, beetroot seeds, melon seeds, pumpkin seeds

It's a good idea to make a pen for your animals. Build one with fences and add a gate, and then lure the animal in with their preferred food. Once they're in, close the gate and feed them. Get two and they'll breed and make new animals, allowing you to get raw meat from the older ones! If you grow attached to some of them you can put them on a leash and tie them to a fence post in order to keep them still, in case you want to go for a walk.

STICKY ELEVATOR!

Want to ride to the top of a cliff in style? Just use some honey blocks!

You may not believe that honey would be a good way to get vertical. Honey blocks are sticky as can be, after all, and prevent you from jumping too high. But they can actually be used to shoot yourself quickly up into the sky!

This build uses the unique properties of soul sand, which actually makes water rise into the air!

WHAT YOU'LL NEED

🟫	**1 SOUL SAND**
🪣	**2 WATER BUCKETS**
🟨	**LOTS OF HONEY BLOCKS**

1

First place a soul stone base on the ground. You'll just need one block for a one-person elevator, more if you want to make a bigger one.

2

Now start adding those sticky honey blocks. Place them on two sides of the soul stone and then build them up into the air.

3

Water Bucket

Once they're up as high as you need them, drop a water bucket right above the soul stone from the top. Ride the water down!

4

Now drop the water bucket at the bottom to add a water source down there, too. If you've done this right you'll start to see bubbles floating up.

5

Here's the fun part! The water is shooting up one way, but go around the structure to look at the honey blocks. Just run into it and jump up and you'll shoot up it! How does that work since the honey is on the other side? The honey blocks are just a little bit smaller than the others, allowing the water to seep through just enough to propel you up.

6

Now you can enjoy the view from the top!

OUR FAVOURITE MINECRAFT CREATIONS

Minecraft's master builders have been making stunning projects for years, and there are seemingly no limits to what people can create in the game. Here are some you have to see to believe!

WORLD OF WORLDS
by Zeemo

Planning a holiday, but just can't figure out where to go next? Why not check out this totally amazing map, which has buildings from 85 cities from all over the world. This is a massive map and every time you turn a corner you're not sure where in the world you're going to visit next. Definitely worth a visit!

BY ZEEMO
WORLD OF WORLDS 3.0

www.minecraftmaps.com/city-maps/world-of-worlds

FROM FLAMES: REBORN
by Gustavo Team

The world has ended, but you survived it in your shelter. Now's your chance to go outside and see what's survived. Save the world by finding a mysterious device and power it with 16 hidden cores. Expect lots of custom weapons, mobs, and loot!

FROM FLAMES:
Reborn

CTM from the Gustavo Team

www.minecraftmaps.com/ctm-maps/from-flames-reborn

MIDNIGHT THOUGHTS
by HeavensGift

Some creations in Minecraft are just made to be admired. This absolute work of art features a jellyfish that looks like it's about to move. It's so well-designed that it's proof of what you can do with just a few simple blocks!

www.planetminecraft.com/project/midnight-thoughts-4195233/

THE ASYLUM
by Sunfury

Ever imagined what Minecraft would be like with scary surprises? Look no further. This dark, spooky map is not for the weak of heart. There are creepy cutscenes, narration, and of course, an utterly disturbing asylum to explore...

www.minecraftmaps.com/horror-maps/the-asylum

FUNLAND 3
by SUPERPISH

It's one thing to make intricate architecture, but it's another to make an actual, functioning amusement park. This place has over 100 different attractions including roller coasters, water rides – even kids rides. There are plenty of secrets too. It's tons of fun for the whole family!

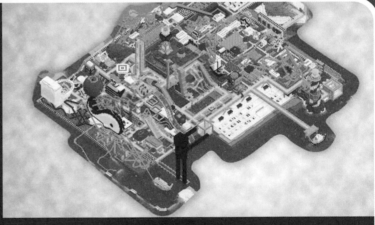

www.minecraftmaps.com/creation-maps/funland-3

ATROPOS
by carloooo

Atropos looks like a neat turtle design... until you take a closer look and realise just how massive it is. This steampunk creation has a level of detail that's just mind-boggling. If you're working on a steampunk world, you're going to want to check this out!

www.planetminecraft.com/project/atropos/

THE BEST MINECRAFT SKINS OF ALL TIME

There are so many awesome avatar skins to choose from, it's hard to know where to start. Here are some of our favourites you can get!

THANOS

Minecraft getting too crowded for you? Download this skin in a snap.

CHEWBACCA

Everyone's favourite furry Star Wars friend has never looked better. Or blockier.

DAENERYS TARGARYEN

For when you want to make your very own Iron Throne, just to burn everything down.

ZOMBIE

Sure, real zombies won't leave you alone if you wear this skin, but it's worth a shot!

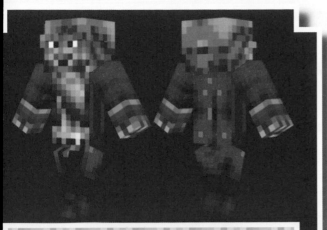

GUYBRUSH THREEPWOOD

Ever played the game Monkey Island? If you can't make a three-headed monkey, you might as well make everyone's favourite pirate.

LINK

We reckon you should all buy or download this legendary elvish outfit.

TV GUY

You can be your very own entertainment with this skin! Note: TV remote not included.

GREEN KNIGHT

You may not get any benefit from wearing this knight's armour, but you sure will look cool.

TRON

Want to play a game inside a game? Here's the best outfit for that.

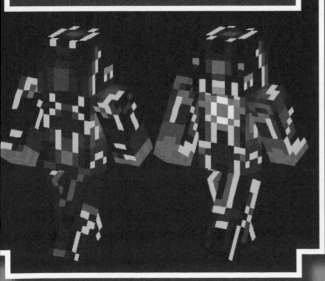

ELSA

Take over all of those frozen biomes and become the ice queen!

MINECRAFT CLASSIC

PLAY THE ORIGINAL IN YOUR BROWSER

Do you miss watching your friends run around, windmilling their arms the way they used to when Minecraft first launched? Then play Minecraft Classic! This is the original version of Minecraft, made available online for free, right in your web browser.

While the things you do here won't transfer over to the main game, it can be pretty fun to see how Minecraft used to be. It's a much more simple and streamlined game, plus, did we mention it's completely free?

Just head to *classic.minecraft.net* and it will randomly generate a new world. You can even invite your friends to play with you. You'll have to copy the link and send it to them, and up to nine buddies can join you for your retro blocky adventure.

Game generated!

You are the host. You can invite some (9) friends to join you.

/classic.minecraft.net/?join=7k-55Bc3N

Copy

Pick a username and start the game.

Creeper | Start

Left click to place or mine blocks (right click to toggle).

Generating level

Raising..

Since there are no enemies, this basically works as Creative mode in the main game. There's no way to die, so use it to create whatever content you like.

REASONS TO PLAY CLASSIC MINECRAFT:

- ✕ You have a few minutes free and you're on a public computer.

- ✕ You want to see how the game used to look years ago.

- ✕ You have an idea for a quick build. Building is so much faster here!

THINGS YOU WON'T FIND HERE:

AN INFINITE WORLD. Classic's map is a cube that's surrounded by infinite water and bedrock.

OBJECTIVES OR UNLOCKS. You just make up your own game!

MOBS. Don't expect to see any animal life!

HEALTH! You can't die, so swim around in lava all you want.

UPDATES. This game will never see another update – it is what it is.

DID YOU KNOW?

Minecraft Classic was the original version, released two years before the game actually came out!

It was originally named 'Minecraft Alpha'.

Blocks don't always work as you'd expect. Experiment to see what's changed!

The water physics are a little... off. Try flooding an entire map with one block of water to see what happens.

MINECRAFT EARTH

Ever wanted to play Minecraft on the go? You may have mobile versions of the game, but have you ever walked around the real world and wish it were more like Minecraft? Enter Minecraft Earth

GET WALKING

As with other AR (Augmented Reality) games, this isn't a great title for couch potatoes. Minecraft Earth will only be fun for those who love to walk around their neighborhoods. Using your phone or tablet, you'll see an in-game map (of your real-world setting) to explore and find 'Tappable' resources to collect and craft. Team up with friends to create incredible showpieces and enjoy the life-sized creations in the world around you. There are even survival adventures to find.

WHAT ARE TAPPABLES?

They are what they sound like. Simply tap on a tappable and you'll gain resources, ranging from mobs to terrain, trees and chest. What you get inside is determined by what type it is — tap on a tree and you'll likely get wood. You may even luck out and get rare resources. Collect the assets in your inventory and you'll be ready to craft them into new items and begin building!

CHARACTER CREATION

As you'd expect, you can customise your character any way you like. There are all kinds of eyes, skin colours, and facial features to choose from, as well as lots of clothes that you can buy for free. There are, of course, some items that can only be purchased with Rubies (the game's currency), which cost real-world money.

Also, if you have a favourite character from the main game, you can just transfer them over!

BUILDPLATES

This is where the game really shines and where you can build anything you like and bring it into the real world. Invite your friends to interact with your Buildplate and you'll be able to expand and experience your structure to life-size, moving around it and adding and removing blocks. These are your own personal creations, so customise them however you like.

OFF TO ADVENTURE!

Adventures are shown on the in-game map as shinning beacons and they are the game's version of Survival Mode; with small pieces of the Minecraft world appearing directly in front of you on the ground! These adventures will earn you extra items and resources – just make sure you are equipped to deal with them!

BUILDING A CHALLENGE

There are daily, weekly, career and event challenges to complete, from collecting mobs or blocks to locating items, such as cobblestone or swords. Each challenge gives you a chance to earn lots of cool items and XP. The best way to level up is to keep checking the challenges menu and try to complete as many as you can.

MINECRAFT DUNGEONS

A LOOK AT THE FIRST NEW GAME FROM MOJANG SINCE MINECRAFT!

AVAILABLE ON: PC, NINTENDO SWITCH, PLAYSTATION 4, XBOX ONE, AND XBOX GAME PASS
RELEASE DATE: SPRING 2020

Love Minecraft, but hate building? Then the all-new adventure game Minecraft Dungeons might be for you! Mojang's first game since Minecraft is a dungeon crawler where you can team up in groups of four to fight enemies and loot treasure.

DELVE DOWN

As you'd expect from the name, you're going to spend a lot of time heading underground into dungeons and crypts. There's a ton of combat involved, with all of the familiar mobs you'd expect and some new ones as well. What's more, the levels are made up of rooms that are randomly-generated, meaning that each level will be different every single time you play!

PLAY AS YOU LIKE

Unlike other dungeon crawlers, you can change the way you play Minecraft Dungeons on the fly just by choosing what to equip. Put on heavy armor and your defense will increase at the expense of making you slower. Equip light armor and you'll become weak yet nimble, allowing you to keep enemies at a distance and attack them with bows and arrows. You can even become a powerful magic-user through the use of equippable artifacts that allow you to cast spells!

P2 Picked Up **Wolf Armor**

P1 Picked Up **Axe**

SWIFTNESS POTION
Briefly boosts movement speed.
Pick Up   A

LEVEL UP!

As you progress, you'll find a lot of loot to aid you in your quest. There are single use supplies, such as food to heal you and TNT to blow up mobs, along with gear that will protect and make you stronger. This includes armour and weapons, which have different enchantments options to make them special and change their abilities. Finally, there are emeralds to collect which can be used to buy weapons or upgrade old items.

CO-OP

Friends can help you, and since this is Minecraft you can bet that there's couch co-op. Friends can jump into your game at any point and the game will automatically make it harder or easier depending on how many players there are. Players can get knocked down if they lose all their health and your friends can revive you, so it's important to stick together. The more friends, the more fun!

A SPECTACULAR
FIREWORKS DISPLAY!

Before you design your display, you'll have to craft some fireworks.

FIREWORK ROCKET (NO EXPLOSION)
Combine gunpowder and paper. The rocket shoots up but doesn't explode. Add additional gunpowder to make it fly higher!

FIREWORK STAR
An element for fireworks. Make them by combining gunpowder with any colour dye. Add additional dyes to make it explode in all different colours. Add seven if you want a rainbow!

FIREWORK ROCKET (LOADED WITH FIREWORK STAR)
Combine a Firework Star with gunpowder and paper for the explosive effect we expect from fireworks!

Along with these basic fireworks you can also add additional items to create special effects!

Now that you have a stockpile of fireworks on hand, it's time to chain them together to explode in a glorious display. Because no one wants to see just one measly firework going off — they want to see non-stop explosions!

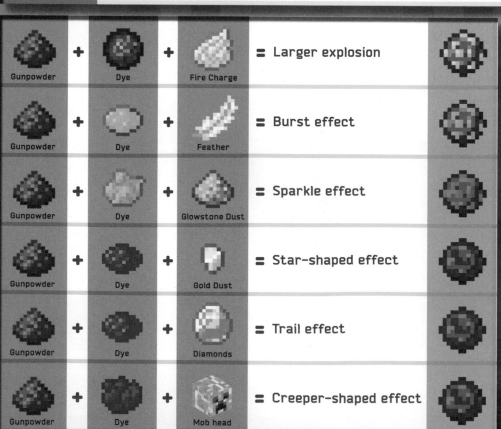

Gunpowder	+	Dye	+	Fire Charge	= Larger explosion	
Gunpowder	+	Dye	+	Feather	= Burst effect	
Gunpowder	+	Dye	+	Glowstone Dust	= Sparkle effect	
Gunpowder	+	Dye	+	Gold Dust	= Star-shaped effect	
Gunpowder	+	Dye	+	Diamonds	= Trail effect	
Gunpowder	+	Dye	+	Mob head	= Creeper-shaped effect	

1

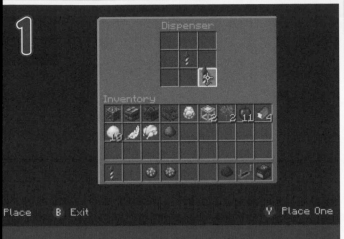

For this you'll need a lever, dispensers, and, most importantly, redstone. Lots of redstone. Simply fill up the dispensers with fireworks, wire them up to the lever with redstone dust, and flip it to set things off.

2

DISPENSERS – These containers can be filled with all sorts of items. They have nine slots of inventory space that can be filled up with fireworks for your display!

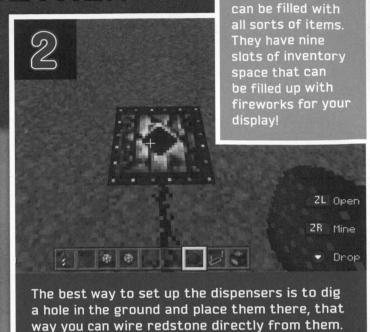

The best way to set up the dispensers is to dig a hole in the ground and place them there, that way you can wire redstone directly from them.

3

Redstone repeaters are a necessity to make a big build, as they extend the current over the dust's normal limit of 5 blocks. Add multiple repeaters together to create a delay, which can be used to space out your fireworks! Timing is everything during a fireworks extravaganza, so you'll want to experiment to see what looks best. Try different types of fireworks and different timings, to see what looks best.

4

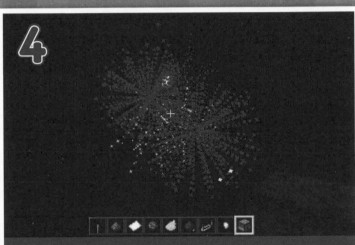

The last step is the most important – wait until dark! Fireworks are basically useless during the day, but the colours really pop at night. Now test your creation and see how it works, tweaking it until it's perfect. Have a blast!

REDSTONE – Redstone dust can be placed on the ground to create Redstone Wire, which can carry a charge between objects. Wire all your dispensers together to a lever and when you flip that lever they'll all go off, allowing you to sit back and enjoy.

REDSTONE REPEATERS – Redstone wire will only carry a charge over a few blocks, so for a big display you'll need repeaters. These will help carry the charge over long distances. You can use them to delay signals as well, changing the timing of your fireworks display!

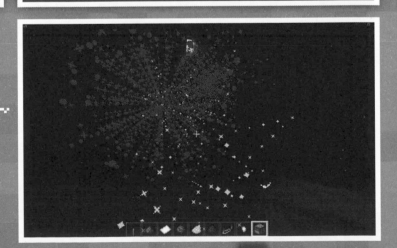

PRO TIP
If you want to get really crazy, you can use repeaters to cause the fireworks to explode to the beat of your favourite songs!

EASTER EGGS

YOU NEVER KNEW

Minecraft is full of all sorts of hidden secrets to find. See how many of these you know!

THE PERILS OF THE VILLAGERS

Villagers are very weak to lots of things. Did you know that if lightning strikes near them, they'll transform into a witch? Zombies can turn them into more zombies as well, but fortunately you can cure them with the combo of a splash potion and a golden apple. It will take a few minutes, but they'll soon come back to life.

MOB HEADS

If a creeper explodes a mob, it'll sometimes drop a head! It sounds yucky, but you can use it as a disguise. Wear them and reduce the chance of that mob detecting you by 50%!

BATS LOVE HALLOWEEN

If you want to find bats outside of caves, play the game at the perfect time. From October 20th through November 3rd bats are more likely to fly around in the light!

MOOSHROOM STEW

In the Mushroom biomes you can find these strange red and black cows that have mushrooms growing all over them! If you shear them they'll turn back into normal cows, but if you milk them they will give you bowls of mushroom stew!

THE AMAZING TECHNICOLOUR SHEEPCOAT

Use an anvil to make a name tag that says 'jeb_', and the sheep you place it on will do something cool - its wool will cycle through every single color known to Minecraft. Sadly, if you shear this wool it will just be normal wool!

LUCKY RABBIT'S FOOT

Once in a while rabbits will drop a rabbit's foot when killed. Brew this with an awkward potion and you'll create a potion of leaping, which lets you jump higher and prevents fall damage!

UNLUCKY BUNNY

Sometimes bunnies aren't so happy-go-lucky. While they're rare, you can sometimes come across killer bunnies. They're easily identified by their white fur and red eyes. Stay far far away from them!

BLAST-PROOF HOMES

Creepers keep destroying your house? Try building it with obsidian. It's not easy to harvest, but explosions won't bother this tough material.

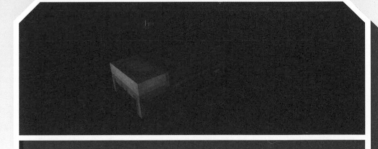

A DEAD LANGUAGE

The runes language that you see for enchantments is called the 'Standard Galactic Alphabet', and was actually taken from the classic Commander Keen series!

THERE'S NO SLEEP AT THE END

Feeling drowsy in the Nether or End? Don't try laying down in a bed. There are explosive consequences for that. Maps don't work either!

A WATERY SAVE

Fall off a cliff? On your way to your imminent death? If you have a bucket of water you can save yourself! Use it at the last second and you'll end up in the water and not die.

PRAISE OUR CHICKEN OVERLORDS

Ever notice that a chicken is always lurking in the back of hostile mobs? Could the chicken be the ringleader behind these evil actions?

MINECRAFT TRIVIA

The End was originally going to be placed in the sky, where you'd fight the dragon on flying islands. The problem was the game engine couldn't handle it, so they made it easier by taking the sun out. It goes to show you, sometimes limitations help creativity!

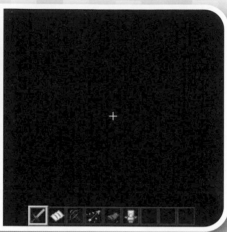

Creepers were created by accident. They were trying to make a pig, but mixed up the numbers for height and length, making this weird (and now iconic) creation.

The alpha of Minecraft was created in just six days.

The sound of Ghasts is actually Minecraft music producer C418's sleeping cat waking up!

A documentary by 2 Player Productions called Minecraft: The Story of Mojang was kickstarted in 2012, and raised over £150,000!

Listen to the Enderman closely and you'll hear that some of its strange language is actually English, pitched way down or played backwards.

Minecraft's original title was Cave Game.

In 2015 Mojang collected an army of Steves. There were 337 of them!

Every time you start up Minecraft, there's a one in 10,000 chance that the name of the game will be misspelled as Minceraft.

There is a World Boundary if you travel far and long, but you can bypass it. There are also two more borders past it, but if you get past the third one, the game will crash.